Contents

Unit 1

When we talk about just one of something we use the **singular** form of a word.

Example: one **worm**

When we want to talk about more than one we use the **plural** form of a word.

Example: six **worms**

To form the plural of most words just add "s".

Example: one car . . . two car**s**   one room . . . many room**s**

1 Form plurals of the following words by adding "s".

one tank / three ....*tanks*............   one drum / several ....

one star / a sky full of ....   one path / two ....

one axe / three ....   one team / four ....

one rule / a book of ....   one page / ten ....

one bike / three ....   one tunnel / two ....

one cage / six ....   one animal / many ....

one field / four ....   one farmer / a group of ....

one mother / many ....   one shed / several ....

2 Complete the sentences with the plurals of the words in brackets.

a (shell) We collected lots of ....*shells*........... at the beach yesterday.

b (teacher) There are eight .... at my school.

c (bike) Ten .... were leaning against the wall.

d (goal) My team scored three ....

e (banana, watermelon) We ate six .... and two ....

f (rabbit, cage) There were many .... in the ....

English Skills

1

Writing
and
Vocabulary

John Barwick
Jenny Barwick

OXFORD
UNIVERSITY PRESS

Introduction

The *English Skills* series is designed to promote and support the development of a high standard of English language use, an essential asset for academic success, and success in the world beyond school.

The series contains two strands:

> *Writing and Vocabulary* (Books 1–3)
> *Writing and Grammar* (Books 1–3)

The books provide teachers with a comprehensive program in English skills, and are also suitable for home use. A pull-out answer section is located in the middle of the book.

In keeping with the recent renewed emphasis on the explicit teaching of language and grammar skills, this series provides coverage of English skills in reading and writing, grammar and vocabulary, spelling and punctuation.

Writing and Vocabulary focuses on essential spelling rules, vocabulary content, and writing skills to provide a strong foundation for successful academic writing. There are a wide variety of activity types and all activities have the following goals:

GOAL   Develop and reinforce knowledge and recall of basic spelling rules and letter patterns

GOAL   Provide practice in useful spelling strategies

GOAL   Build vocabulary knowledge and recall

GOAL   Promote student confidence and independent work

Many activities incorporate content from curriculum areas such as mathematics, social studies, and the natural world.

Look out for common letter patterns. The letter pattern "ew" is found in many words.

1 Circle all the words in the snake which contain the letter pattern "ew". Write them below.

blewwooddrewgaragechewflewdinosaurgrewwavedewsizewidestewapartfewalivelistpewfearthrewtruebl/qnawau

.............blew............. ....

....

....

....

2 Choose the correct "ew" word from the box to complete the sentences.

new   cashew   nephew   crew

a Rebecca rode her ....*new*........ bike to school today.

b The .... of the ship did not panic in the storm.

c My uncle says I am his favorite ....

d My father loves eating .... nuts.

Unit 3

| For **plurals** of words ending in "s", "ss", "x", or "z", add "es". ||
Singular	Plural
one **bus**	two **buses**
one **waltz**	three **waltzes**
one **fox**	two **foxes**

1   Add "es" to these words to make them plural.

one bus / three..........*buses*.............   one guess / three ....

one pass / a few.............................   one class / four..

one glass / a tray of.........................   one miss / two ....

one princess / three........................ .   one boss / two ....

one waltz / six.............................. .   one fox / many..

one box / three............................. .   one mattress / ten ....

2   Complete the sentences with the plurals of the words
in brackets.

a   (box) We put the...........*boxes*.......... on the floor.

b   (fox) I saw six .... near my house yesterday.

c   (loss) My team had nine wins and five ....

d   (rhino) A few .... were stomping through the grass.

e   (tax) Everyone has to pay their ....

4

> **Homophones** are words that sound the same, but have different spellings and different meanings.
>
> | bare/bear | The cabinet was **bare**.
I saw a **bear** at the zoo. |
> |---|---|
> | sun/son | The **sun** was shining brightly.
The woman took her **son** to school. |
> | hear/here | I can **hear** a strange noise.
I came **here** about two hours ago. |

1 Choose the correct word to complete the sentences.

a (sun/son) The..............*sun*............ always rises in the east.

b (sun/son) "My .... has just scored a goal," said Mr Gibbs.

c (bean/been) There was only one jelly .... left in the jar.

d (bean/been) I have never .... to France.

e (meat/meet) The .... is in the fridge.

f (meat/meet) "I will .... you at the shop in five minutes," said Julia.

g (buy/by) "Let's .... some ice cream in the park," said Dad.

h (buy/by) Ben is standing .... the door.

i (hear/here) "I can .... someone shouting," said Rani.

j (hear/here) "Put your bags over ....," said our teacher.

Writing

2 Fix the mistakes in this sentence.

Wen we were at the zoo we saw some dear.

....

| For **plurals** of words ending in "ch", add "es". ||
Singular	**Plural**
one **coach**	two **coaches**
one **beach**	three **beaches**
one **bench**	four **benches**

1   **Form plurals by adding "es".**

one lunch / four......_lunches_..........   one beach / two ....

one peach / a box of......................   one bench / five ....

one catch / three ....   one pouch / ten ....

one speech / two ....   one church / a few.........................

one scratch / lots of.......................   one watch / six ....

one couch / three.........................   one ostrich / several......................

2   **Complete the sentences below with the plurals of the words in brackets.**

a   (batch) We made three....._batches_..... of scones.

b   (branch) There were lots of .... on the ground after the strong winds.

c   (crutch) Lauren has to use .... for three weeks while her ankle heals.

d   (latch) The .... on all the doors were broken.

e   (coach, match) The .... of the four teams agreed to cancel the ....

6

Numbers word search

Find the numbers listed in the box. Write each word on the lines.

one	two	three	~~four~~	five	six	seven	eight
nine	ten	twenty	thirty	forty	fifty		

t	h	r	e	e	l	h	t
h	t	y	t	r	a	w	h
g	s	s	e	v	e	n	i
i	k	i	k	n	o	y	r
e	i	x	t	n	o	w	t
t	w	y	f	o	r	t	y
o	n	e	i	o	u	r	f
r	s	o	f	o	u	h	i
t	h	i	t	e	n	r	v
w	o	n	y	n	i	n	e

four

....

....

....

....

....

....

....

....

....

....

....

7

For **plurals** of words ending in "sh", add "es".	
Singular	Plural
one **brush**	two **brushes**
one **bush**	three **bushes**
one **dish**	a stack of **dishes**

1 Form plurals by adding "es".

one wish / two ....*wishes*..........

one toothbrush / five ....

one smash / three ....

one eyelash / Jessica"s...................

one polish / several.......................

one radish / a few ....

one push / a couple of ....

one crash / three...............................

one splash / many big ....

one paintbrush / six............................

one wash / many...............................

one bush / several ....

2 Complete the sentences with the plurals of the words in brackets.

a (bush) We were hiding behind some ......*bushes*.......

b (paintbrush) John found three .... in the garage.

c (flash) A few .... of lightning lit up the sky.

d (dish) There are three .... on the table.

e (marsh) The animals escaped into some ....

Unit 8

Look out for common letter patterns. The letter pattern "ck" is found in many words.

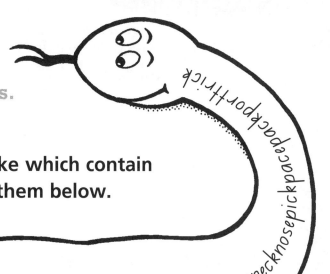

1 Circle all the words in the snake which contain the letter pattern "ck". Write them below.

stackninesockthattherockblockboxcrackcarrydeckwasteamhikekicksportsackwarmsizenecknosepickpacdarportHrick

.............stack............ ....

....

....

....

2 Choose the correct "ck" word from the box to complete the sentences.

| ~~sick~~ lock black sticky neck |

a Yuki wasn't at school today because she was ....sick.......

b My dog has .... ears and a spot on his ....

c Our hands were .... from the juice from

the oranges.

d The .... on the door was broken.

Unit 9

For **plurals** of words ending in "ay", "ey", or "oy", add "s".

Singular form	Plural form
one **day**	two **days**
one **pulley**	three **pulleys**
one **boy**	a group of **boys**

1 **Form plurals by adding "s".**

one way / two .... _ways_ ....   one key / a bunch of ....

one monkey / a group of ....   one toy / a few ....

one bay / four ....   one tray / two................................

one ray / several bright ....   one donkey / several.......................

one play / three ....   one holiday / a few ....

one valley / two...........................   one chimney / three ....

2 **Complete the sentences with the plurals of the words in brackets.**

a (boy) There were three ...._boys_........ and two girls in the classroom.

b (convoy) Three .... of trucks made their way into town.

c (trolley) A few .... were still in the parking lot.

d (highway) Two major .... run through the town.

e (delay) There were only short .... at the gates on both days of the show.

Find the animal words listed in the box. Write each word on the lines.

shark	worm	dinosaur	~~duck~~	bear	horse	kitten
snake	zebra	frog	chicken	tiger	mouse	koala

m	d	i	n	o	s	a	u	r	e
x	t	u	y	r	e	g	i	t	s
w	l	m	c	m	h	g	m	y	u
s	h	a	r	k	o	v	o	m	o
h	q	r	w	o	r	m	n	r	m
a	m	m	o	a	s	d	e	k	f
r	l	p	m	l	e	v	t	o	h
b	r	b	e	a	r	x	t	a	s
e	z	b	n	e	k	c	i	h	c
z	n	l	o	s	n	a	k	e	t

...............*duck*...............

....

....

....

....

....

....

....

....

....

....

....

11

Unit 11

For **plurals** of words ending with consonants followed by "y", change the "y" to "i" and add "es".

Singular form	Plural form
one **cherry**	two **cherries**
one **ferry**	three **ferries**
one **lady**	four **ladies**

1   **Form plurals by changing "y" to "i" and adding "es".**

one party / three.........._parties_.......   one fairy / lots of ....

one family / five ....   one lady / a group of ....

one fly / several ....   one pony / six...............................

one city / two ....   one berry / a bowl of......................

one butterfly / three.......................   one body / two.............................

one baby / four ....   one dairy / a few...........................

2   **Complete the sentences with the plurals of the words in brackets.**

a   (hobby) My favorite....._hobbies_.... are reading and making models.

b   (mummy) The museum has several Egyptian .... on display.

c   (cherry) I eat .... every day. I love them!

d   (spy) The .... in the movie were wearing black suits.

e   (battery) My toy wouldn't work because both .... were dead.

Follow the steps below to practice spelling new and tricky words.

Look carefully at the word.

Say the word and **listen** as you say it.

Cover the word with something.

Write the word.

Check your spelling.

Practice spelling the following words.

holiday	.... *holiday*	know	....
break	....	library	....
writing	....	useful	....
voice	....	rescue	....
argue	....	allow	....
enjoy	....	prepare	....
arrive	....	through	....
square	....	always	....
dinosaur	....	piece	....
friend	....	country	....
rough	....	surprise	....

For **plurals** of some words ending in "f" or "fe", change the "f" to "v" and add "es".

Singular	Plural
one **half**	two **halves**
one **loaf**	four **loaves**

1 **Write the plurals of the words.**

one wolf / a pack of ......*wolves*......   one life / several ....

one wife / a group of ....   one leaf / five ....

one shelf / four ....   one knife / three ....

For **plurals** of some words ending in "f" or "fe", just add "s".

Singular	Plural
one **gulf**	two **gulfs**
one **life**	Nine **lives**

2 **Form the plurals of the following words by adding "s".**

one reef / three ....*reefs*...........   one chief / five ....

one cuff / two..............................   one puff / three...........................

one cliff / three ....   one giraffe / five.........................

For **plurals** of some words ending in "f" or "fe", it can be done **both ways.** Your choice!

Singular	Plural
one **dwarf**	a group of **dwarves**
	a group of **dwarfs**

3 **Write both plural forms of the words.**

one dwarf / five.............................   ....

one hoof / four.............................   ....

Unit 14

Synonyms and antonyms 1

> **Synonyms** are words with the same or similar meanings.
>
> **Large** and **big** are synonyms. They have the same meaning.
>
> **Hat** and **cap** are synonyms too.

1   **Match the words from the box with their synonyms.**

little	push	~~close~~	fast	damp
mend	soft	stick	rush	reply

shut   ....*close*...............   wet   ....

fix   ....   small   ....

answer   ....   shove   ....

hurry   ....   gentle   ....

hurry   ....   twig   ....

> **Antonyms** are words with opposite meanings.
>
> **Large** and **small** are antonyms. They have opposite meanings.
>
> **Stand up** and **sit down** are antonyms too.

2   **Match the words from the box with their antonyms.**

start	~~easy~~	in	blunt	slow
float	lost	front	hot	dark

hard   ....*easy*...............   back   ....

out   ....   fast   ....

light   ....   cold   ....

found   ....   end   ....

sharp   ....   sink   ....

15

> For some **irregular plurals,** change some letters in the word's singular form.
>
> | one **woman** | four **women** |
> |---|---|
> | one **foot** | two **feet** |

1 Write the plurals of the words.

one tooth / three .... *teeth* ....   one child / several ....

one goose / a flock of.....................   one mouse / lots of ....

one foot / my two.........................   one man / a group of ....

> For some **irregular plurals,** use the same form as the singular.
>
> | one **sheep** | seven **sheep** |
> |---|---|
> | one **fish** | ten **fish** |

2 Write the plurals of the words.

one fish / a bucket full of .... *fish* ....   one deer / a few ....

one trout / six.................................   one salmon / lots of.................

3 Circle the correct form of plural for each of the words.

woman	womans / ⟨women⟩
child	children / childs
cat	cats / cat
mouse	mouses / mice
deer	deer / deers
hamster	hamster / hamsters
foot	feet / foots
sheep	sheep / sheeps

Letter patterns 3

English has many common letter patterns. The letter pattern "dr" is found in many words.

1 Circle all the words in the snake which contain the letter pattern "dr". Write them below.

drilloflakedrivefencedrybgatedragonmapdropfooldraindressandrinkpersondrumherddramadeepdreamandrkdrayday

.............*drill*.............. ....

....

....

....

2 Choose the correct "dr" word from the box to complete the sentences.

drawing	drums	~~drag~~	dragon	drop

a The box was so heavy I had to.........*drag*........ it along the ground.

b He's .... a picture of a house with a pencil.

c I had a scary dream about a big red ....

d My brother plays the .... in a band.

e Be careful with that box. Don't .... it!

Write the correct plural form.

familys / families.......*families*.......

mice / mouses ....

vallies / valleys ....

beaches / beachs ....

teacheres / teachers ....

reefs / reeves ....

tooths / teeth ....

waltzs / waltzes ....

monkeys / monkies ....

flashes / flashs ....

trayes / trays ....

cityes / cities................................

watchies / watches ....

hoofes / hoofs ....

bananaes / bananas ....

holidaies / holidays.........................

guess's / guesses ....

sheep / sheeps...............................

animales / animals...............................

knives / knifes ....

brushes / brushs ....

class's / classes ....

teames / teams ....

berrys / berries ....

bus's / buses ....

torchs / torches..................................

wolfs / wolves ....

lives / lifes................................... .

chiefs / chieves ....

fish / fishs ....

children / childs..................................

ponys / ponies.....................................

batterys / batteries..............................

womans / women ....

foxs / foxes..

crashs / crashes ....

18

Homophones are words which sound the same but have different spellings and mean different things.

Homophones are words that sound the same, but have different spellings and different meanings.

for/four	We ate pancakes **for** breakfast. I saw **four** cars on the road.
sale/sail	The shop has a big **sale** next week. The **sail** on the small boat is white.

1   **Choose the correct word to complete the sentences.**

a   (sale/sail) The house on the corner is for............*sale*.........

b   (sale/sail) The boat's .... was torn in the wind.

c   (two/to/too) "May I have some ice cream, ...?" asked Lucy.

d   (two/to/too) I went .... Thailand last year.

e   (two/to/too) There are .... books on the table.

f   (weak/week) It's my birthday next ....

g   (weak/week) Su-hee was too .... to get out of bed because she was sick.

h   (pair/pear) There is a .... of boots next to the door.

i   (pair/pear) Jamie ate the last ....

j   (sea/see) The .... was clear, blue, and beautiful.

k   (sea/see) I can't .... the ball anywhere.

Writing

2   **Rewrite the sentence with all words spelled correctly.**

May I have a peace of cake, pleese?

....

Unit 19

Silent "e"	
Words without a silent "e" at the end usually have **short** vowel sounds. Words with a silent "e" at the end usually have **long** vowel sounds.	
Short vowel sounds	**Long vowel sounds**
not	note
hat	hate
pet	Pete

1   Add a silent "e" to the following. Write the new word. Say each pair of words.

strip   ....stripe............   tap   ....

rod   ....   shin   ....

mop   ....   mat   ....

rip   ....   hop   ....

cap   ....   pal   ....

2   Choose the correct word to complete the sentences.

a   (tape/tap) Make sure you turn the...........tap.......... off properly.

b   (tape/tap) This roll of .... is nearly used up.

c   (Hop/Hope) "........................... to the end of the line," said Mr. Malone.

d   (hop/hope) I .... it doesn't rain today.

e   (ripe/rip) Be careful not to .... the paper.

f   (ripe/rip) I don't think this banana is .... yet.

g   (shin/shine) The ball hit me on the ....

h   (shin/shine) .... those shoes with this brush.

Shape and space word search

Find the shape and space words listed in the box. Write each word on the lines.

square	triangle	round	rectangle	solid	base
corner	graph	position	sharp	blunt	circle

r	e	c	t	a	n	g	l	e
o	d	i	l	o	s	r	u	v
u	t	r	i	a	n	g	l	e
n	n	c	o	r	n	e	r	n
d	u	l	b	g	b	a	s	e
h	l	e	l	q	u	a	o	s
p	b	l	s	q	u	a	s	h
a	e	l	s	e	c	a	f	a
r	o	d	l	i	n	g	r	r
g	n	o	i	t	i	s	o	p

.... *square* ....

....

....

....

....

....

....

....

....

....

....

Hurry up, we don't have all day!

Unit 21

Present tense verbs	
For many verbs in present tense, add "s" when used with **he** or **she**.	
I **eat**	He/She **eats**
jump	**jumps**
live	**lives**

1 Add "s" to the following verbs.

happen	*happens*	hold	....
cheer	....	shine	....
mark	....	sing	....
give	....	buy	....
scare	....	move	....
decide	....	close	....
listen	....	play	....
expect	....	change	....
arrive	....	invite	....

2 Add "s" to the following verbs.

a (drive) Dad usually ....*drives*........ me to school on Saturday.

b (wake) My dog .... me every morning.

c (smell) This room .... of burnt toast.

d (agree) Joel .... with me that the movie was great.

e (contain) The box .... photos.

Look out for common letter patterns. The letter pattern "cl" begins many words.

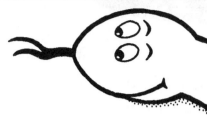

1 Circle all the words in the snake which begin with the letter pattern "cl". Write them below.

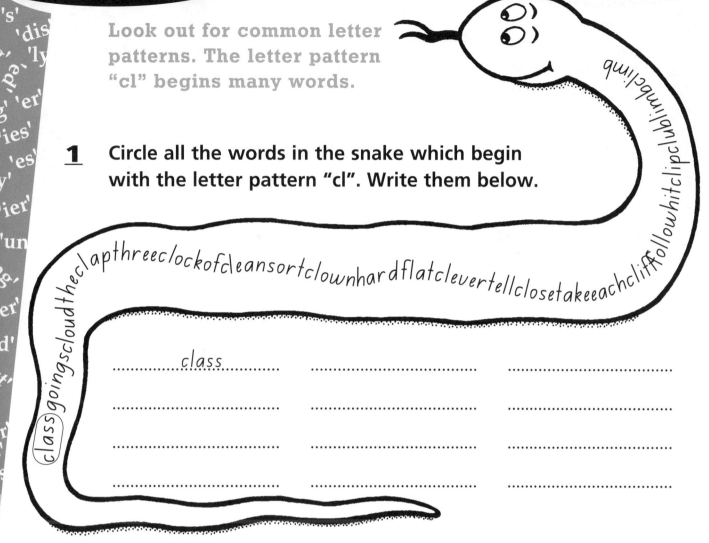

.... *class* ....

....

....

....

2 Choose the correct "cl" word from the box to complete the sentences.

claws   ~~clink~~   clay   clear

a There was a.......... *clink* .... as the money fell down the grate.

b We used .... to make a pot.

c There are no clouds today. It's a .... day.

d The bird's .... were very sharp.

Unit 23

Present tense verbs
Use "am", "is", or "are", then add "ing" to the verb to describe an action that happens **now**.

I **eat** spaghetti.	I **am eating** pizza.
She **plays** tennis.	She **is playing** golf.
We **go** to Boston.	We **are going** to Seoul.

1 Add "ing" to the following verbs.

fold ....folding..........   mend ....

lift ....   bump ....

bring ....   cross ....

dress ....   draw ....

kick ....   meet ....

finish ....   say ....

teach ....   collect ....

swing ....   hurry ....

2 Add "ing" to the following verbs.

a (catch) We are ......catching...... a bus to the store.

b (warn) There is a sign .... people not to go close to the edge.

c (train) I am .... my parrot to talk.

d (ask) Angela is .... her mother if she can come to my house.

e (wash) Emma is .... her car.

Find the farm words listed in the box. Write each word on the lines.

farm	wool	shed	paddock	plant	tractor	farmer
sheep	tank	field	crop	harvest	goat	fence

p	m	c	t	r	a	c	t	o	r
e	j	r	e	m	r	a	f	p	m
s	h	o	y	r	m	j	e	m	f
h	e	p	s	a	t	e	m	g	a
e	c	n	e	f	h	m	o	o	r
d	t	m	m	s	i	u	t	a	m
a	n	h	a	r	v	e	s	t	r
t	a	n	k	l	s	r	l	l	o
m	l	o	o	w	j	p	q	d	s
o	p	a	d	d	o	c	k	b	m

sheep

....

....

....

....

....

....

....

....

....

....

....

Unit 25

Past tense verbs	
Add "ed" to regular verbs for past actions.	
She **plays** tennis.	She **played** tennis yesterday.
I **watch** TV.	I **watched** TV last night.
He **stays** here.	He **stayed** here last month.

1 Add "ed" to the following verbs.

rush ....rushed..........   dust ....

crack ....   thank ....

cheer ....   roar ....

act ....   push ....

clean ....   comb ....

pack ....   float ....

allow ....   reach ....

kick ....   present ....

2 Add "ed" to the following verbs.

a (splash) The water ....splashed..... over the side of the boat.

b (dash) We .... inside when it began to rain.

c (rocket) The bike .... down the slope.

d (pass) The train .... through the station without stopping.

e (call) I .... my friend Yoshi on the phone yesterday.

Syllables		
Breaking up words into chunks can help you spell and pronounce them correctly.		
One syllable	**Two syllables**	**Three syllables**
cat	goldfish	computer
jump	hurry	expensive
run	notebook	library
small	little	register

I can break any word into chunks!

Put the words from the box in the correct list.

| forget   huge   Saturday   always   insect   bright |
| somebody   afternoon   wrap   kangaroo   thirsty   family |
| either   throw   anything   contain   friend   clean |
| piece   chance   people   answer   banana   yesterday |

One-syllable words	Two-syllable words	Three-syllable words
huge	forget	Saturday
....	....	....
....	....	....
....	....	....
....	....	....
....	....	....
....	....	....
....	....	....

Unit 27

Adding "ing" to verbs ending in "e"	
For actions happening now, drop the "e" before adding "ing".	
wipe	He's **wiping** the table now.
skate	She's **skating** on the ice now.

I'm sick of all this wiping!

1 Add "ing" to the following verbs.

bake ....baking........... race ....

shade .... live ....

hope .... smile ....

make .... slide ....

paste .... choose ....

scare .... dance ....

arrive .... change ....

sharing .... invite ....

2 Add "ing" to the following verbs.

a (write) I am ......writing....... a letter to my cousin.

b (take) Amy's mother is .... me to training.

c (save) Luisa is .... money for her trip to Spain.

d (close) The pool will be .... in half an hour.

e (move) The cars are .... quickly now because the road is open again.

Answers

Unit 1

1 tanks, drums, stars, paths, axes, teams, rules, pages, bikes, tunnels, cages, animals, fields, farmers, mothers, sheds

2 **a** shells **b** teachers **c** bikes **d** goals **e** bananas, watermelons **f** rabbits, cages

Unit 2

1 blew, drew, chew, flew, grew, dew, stew, few, pew, threw, brew, mew

2 **a** a new **b** crew **c** nephew **d** cashew

Unit 3

1 buses, guesses, passes, classes, glasses, misses, princesses, bosses, waltzes, foxes, boxes, mattresses

2 **a** boxes **b** foxes **c** losses **d** rhinos **e** taxes

Unit 4

1 **a** sun **b** son **c** bean **d** been **e** meat **f** meet **g** buy **h** by **i** hear **j** here

2 When we were at the zoo we saw some deer.

Unit 5

1 lunches, beaches, peaches, benches, catches, pouches, speeches, churches, scratches, watches, couches, ostriches

2 **a** batches **b** branches **c** crutches **d** latches **e** coaches, matches

Unit 6

t	h	r	e	e		l	h		t
h	t	y	t	r	a	w	h	
g	s	s	e	v	e	n	i	
i	k	i	k	n	o	y	r	
e	i	x	t	n	o	w	t	
t	w	y	f	o	r	t	y	
o	n	e	i	o	u	r	f	
r	s	o	f	o	u	h	i	
t	h	i	t	e	n	r	v	
w	o	n	y	n	i	n	e	

Unit 7

1 wishes, pushes, toothbrushes, crashes, smashes, splashes, eyelashes, paintbrushes, polishes, washes, radishes, bushes

2 **a** bushes **b** paintbrushes **c** flashes **d** dishes **e** marshes

Unit 8

1 stack, sock, rock, block, crack, deck, kick, sack, neck, pick, pack, trick

2 **a** sick **b** black, neck **c** sticky **d** lock

Unit 9

1 ways, keys, monkeys, toys, bays, trays, rays, donkeys, plays, holidays, valleys, chimneys

2 **a** boys **b** convoys **c** trolleys **d** highways **e** delays

Unit 10

m	d	i	n	o	s	a	u	r	e
x	t	u	y	r	e	g	i	t	s
w	l	m	c	m	h	g	m	y	u
s	h	a	r	k	o	v	o	m	o
h	q	r	w	o	r	m	n	r	m
a	m	m	o	a	s	d	e	k	f
r	l	p	m	l	e	v	t	o	h
b	r	b	e	a	r	x	t	a	s
e	z	b	n	e	k	c	i	h	c
z	n	l	o	s	n	a	k	e	t

Unit 11

1 parties, fairies, families, ladies, flies, ponies, cities, berries, butterflies, bodies, babies, dairies

2 **a** hobbies **b** mummies **c** cherries **d** spies **e** batteries

Unit 12

Check words are spelt correctly.

Unit 13

1 wolves, lives, wives, leaves, shelves, knives

2 reefs, chiefs, cuffs, puffs, cliffs, giraffes

3 **a** dwarfs, dwarves **b** hoofs, hooves

Unit 14

1 close, damp, mend, little, reply, push, rush, soft, fast, stick

2 easy, front, in, slow, dark, hot, lost, start, blunt, float

Answers

Unit 15

1 teeth, children, geese, mice, feet, men

2 fish, deer, trout, salmon

3 women, children, cats, mice, deer, hamsters, feet, sheep

Unit 16

1 drill, drive, dry, dragon, drop, drain, dress, drink, drum, drama, drew, dray

2 **a** drag **b** drawing **c** dragon **d** drums **e** drop

Unit 17

families, animals, mice, knives, valleys, brushes, beaches, classes, teachers, teams, reefs, berries, teeth, buses, waltzes, torches, monkeys, wolves, flashes, lives, trays, chiefs, cities, fish, watches, children, hoofs, ponies, bananas, batteries, holidays, women, guesses, foxes, sheep, crashes

Unit 18

1 **a** sale **b** sail **c** too **d** to **e** two **f** week **g** weak **h** pair **i** pear **j** sea **k** see

2 May I have a piece of cake, please?

Unit 19

1 stripe, tape, rode, shine, mope, mate, ripe, hope, cape, pale

2 **a** tap **b** tape **c** Hop **d** hope **e** rip **f** ripe **g** shin **h** shine

Unit 20

r	e	c	t	a	n	g	l	e
o	d	i	l	o	s	r	u	v
u	t	r	i	a	n	g	l	e
n	n	c	o	r	n	e	r	n
d	u	l	b	g	b	a	s	e
h	l	e	l	q	u	a	o	s
p	b	l	s	q	u	a	s	h
a	e	l	s	e	c	a	f	a
r	o	d	l	i	n	g	r	r
g	n	o	i	t	i	s	o	p

Unit 21

1 happens, holds, cheers, shines, marks, sings, gives, buys, scares, moves, decides, closes, listens, plays, expects, changes, arrives, invites

2 **a** drives **b** wakes **c** smells **d** agrees **e** contains

Unit 22

1 class, cloud, clap, clock, clean, clown, clever, close, cliff, clip, club, climb.

2 **a** clink **b** clay **c** clear **d** claws

Unit 23

1 folding, mending, lifting, bumping, bringing, crossing, dressing, drawing, kicking, meeting, finishing, saying, teaching, collecting, swinging, hurrying

2 **a** catching **b** warning **c** training **d** asking **e** washing

Unit 24

p	m	c	t	r	a	c	t	o	r
e	j	r	e	m	r	a	f	p	m
s	h	o	y	r	m	j	e	m	f
h	e	p	s	a	t	e	m	g	a
e	c	n	e	f	h	m	o	o	r
d	t	m	m	s	i	u	t	a	m
a	n	h	a	r	v	e	s	t	r
t	a	n	k	l	s	r	l	l	o
m	l	o	o	w	j	p	q	d	s
o	p	a	d	d	o	c	k	b	m

Unit 25

1 rushed, dusted, cracked, thanked, cheered, roared, acted, pushed, cleaned, combed, packed, floated, allowed, reached, kicked, presented

2 **a** splashed **b** dashed **c** rocketed **d** passed **e** called

Unit 26

one-syllable words: huge, bright, wrap, throw, friend, clean, piece, chance

two-syllable words: forget, always, insect, thirsty, either, contain, people, answer

three-syllable words: Saturday, somebody, afternoon, kangaroo, family, anything, banana, yesterday

Unit 27

1 baking, racing, shading, living, hoping, smiling, making, sliding, pasting, choosing, scaring, dancing, arriving, changing, sharing, inviting

2 **a** writing **b** taking **c** saving **d** closing **e** moving

Unit 28

1 scare, hit, sparkle, centre, twist, allow, odd, tear, stone, blend

2 over, short, strong, outside, enter, friend, dry, near, top, never

Answers

Unit 29

1 chased, lived, waved, arrived, amazed, snored, liked, invited, hated, shared, decided, rescued, prepared, agreed

2 a scored **b** closed **c** smiled **d** pasted **e** used

Unit 30

1 bread, bridge, break, brush, branch, brother, brown, broom, brave, brick, brew, bride

2 a broccoli **b** breakfast **c** bring **d** bread

Unit 31

1 trying, flying, spraying, saying, laying, tidying, burying, copying, obeying, praying, enjoying, staying, worrying, hurrying, carrying, spying

2 a frying **b** emptying **c** drying **d** terrifying **e** annoying

Unit 32

1 a road **b** rode **c** tale **d** tail **e** ate **f** eight **g** blue **h** blew **i** read **j** red **k** hair **l** hare

2 My dog has a lot of trouble with fleas.

Unit 33

1 stays, stayed; enjoys, enjoyed; obeys, obeyed; play, played; brays, brayed; displays, displayed

2 cries, cried; tries, tried; buries, buried; carries, carried; hurries, hurried; worries, worried; copies, copied

Unit 34

t	h	c	a	p	a	c	i	t	y
e	e	v	h	w	a	r	m	e	r
m	a	r	g	o	l	l	k	a	r
p	v	n	r	e	l	o	o	c	j
e	i	o	j	f	r	e	t	i	l
r	e	t	e	m	i	t	n	e	c
a	r	e	m	a	s	s	n	s	w
t	o	r	e	t	h	g	i	l	t
u	a	r	e	a	t	n	s	i	s
r	r	t	q	h	t	a	m	h	t
e	m	u	l	o	v	e	n	a	s

Unit 35

1 skipped, skipping; flipped, flipping; tripped, tripping; shopped, shopping; stepped, stepping; chipped, chipping; spotted, spotting; drummed, drumming; snapped, snapping; hugged, hugging; ripped, ripping; stopped, stopping

Unit 36

1 sleep, between, cheese, meet, keep, queen, canteen, agree, deep, weep, feel, keen

2 a feed, cheetah **b** need **c** reef **d** free

Unit 37

crashed, crashes, crashing; wrapped, wraps, wrapping; fried, fries, frying; baked, bakes, baking; smiled, smiles, smiling; hurried, hurries, hurrying; dragged, drags, dragging; enjoyed, enjoys, enjoying; shared, shares, sharing; flied, flies, flying; carried, carries, carrying; passed, passes, passing; tripped, trips, tripping; planned, plans, planning; expected, expects, expecting; jumped, jumps, jumping

Unit 38

p	m	g	a	r	d	e	n	s	m
v	o	l	i	b	r	a	r	y	t
a	r	o	b	a	l	m	w	m	e
c	h	a	l	l	m	a	d	r	p
h	c	h	c	i	t	y	v	l	a
u	u	r	s	m	c	z	m	q	r
r	t	m	w	h	t	n	q	n	k
c	s	c	h	o	o	l	u	w	q
h	k	l	a	t	i	p	s	o	h
m	s	c	i	n	e	m	a	t	c

Unit 39

1 windy, sandy, tricky, dusty, hairy, soapy, sugary, salty, sleepy, plucky, frosty, rusty, thirsty, lumpy, woody, cheery

2 a cloudy **b** bloody **c** itchy **d** dirty **e** fishy

Unit 40

c	h	c	h	a	m	o	s	t	m
m	r	e	n	i	m	a	y	o	f
t	e	a	c	h	e	r	y	p	f
s	d	m	p	g	c	m	d	o	a
i	l	r	l	e	h	t	s	l	r
t	i	o	u	s	a	c	i	i	m
n	u	t	m	r	n	b	h	c	e
e	b	c	b	u	i	l	d	e	r
d	m	o	e	n	c	d	m	o	f
h	b	d	r	i	v	e	r	m	y

Unit 41

1 spotty, baggy, starry, muddy, grubby, smoggy, runny, zippy, knotty, nippy, sloppy, starry.

2 a snappy **b** boggy **c** funny **d** blurry

Unit 42

1 powerful, amaze, lock, collect, tired, least, raise, weep

2 catch, shallow, laugh, shout, happy, mend, wrong, on, sunset, present

Answers

Unit 43

1 cheerful, boastful, useful, thoughtful, hopeful, joyful, powerful, painful, respectful, truthful, watchful, peaceful, playful, graceful, forgetful, thankful

2 **a** helpful **b** harmful **c** faithful **d** forkful **e** wonderful

Unit 44

1 load, soap, coat, road, coach, foam, soak, croak, roam, boat, coal.

2 **a** loaf **b** goal **c** moan, goat **d** roast

Unit 45

happier, happiest; dirtier, dirtiest; funnier, funniest; soapier, soapiest; muddier, muddiest; stickier, stickiest; baggier, baggiest; thirstier, thirstiest; sillier, silliest; sleepier, sleepiest; luckier, luckiest; trickier, trickiest

Unit 46

1 **a** flower **b** flour **c** wear **d** where **e** right **f** Write **g** cheep **h** cheap **i** main **j** mane

2 **a** I'm not allowed to come to the party on Tuesday.

Unit 47

1 slowly, quickly, softly, neatly, brightly, thinly, weakly, loosely, boldly, bravely, correctly, cleverly, carefully, suddenly, strongly, clearly

2 **a** a wildly **b** glumly **c** gruffly **d** hopefully **e** proudly

Unit 48

C	A	L	E	N	D	A	R	W	M
L	L	F	H	E	I	E	E	E	O
O	C	O	L	W	G	R	E	A	T
C	U	R	C	M	I	N	U	T	E
R	E	R	M	K	T	I	E	W	Y
C	T	T	O	H	A	L	F	E	A
L	R	B	N	A	L	T	A	E	D
O	A	V	T	D	I	R	G	K	D
C	T	H	H	S	I	N	I	F	I
H	S	T	H	G	I	N	D	I	M

Unit 49

1 isn't, wasn't, didn't, haven't, mustn't, weren't, I'm, I've, here's, there's

2 **a** She's **b** I've **c** There's **d** hasn't **e** He'll **f** That's

Unit 50

t	o	m	y	t	o	t	a	e	m
o	b	e	a	n	i	u	e	m	i
c	a	r	r	o	t	c	m	y	l
a	o	t	a	m	o	t	t	o	k
r	c	r	m	e	y	r	i	d	a
p	h	w	n	l	f	m	t	a	r
e	e	h	c	r	y	l	l	e	j
a	e	j	u	i	c	e	j	r	e
r	s	m	a	n	a	n	a	b	l
m	e	p	e	a	n	u	t	l	y

Unit 51

1 lamb, **write**, **g**host, climb, **knee**, comb, half, **wreck**, hour, thumb, **knock**, numb, **guess**, bomb, **gnaw**, limb

2 lamb, climb, comb, thumb, numb, bomb, limb.

3 half, write, wreck, bomb, knee, limb, guess, numb, hour, comb, lamb, thumb, knock, climb, gnaw, ghost

Unit 52

1 wail, afraid, train, main, nail, wait, chain, bait, contain, fail, sail, hail

2 **a** rain, trail **b** Mail, train **c** stain, remained **d** sailed

Unit 53

1 bathroom, sunburn, flashlight, homework, workbook, toothbrush, fingernail, footprint, overcoat, flagpole, lifeboat, raincoat, sunglasses, lifesaver, buttonhole, sandpaper

2 **a** lifeboat, lifesaver **b** workbook, homework **c** overcoat, raincoat

3 toe, toenail

Unit 54

a ten **b** fin **c** lad **d** war **e** ape **f** pal **g** wing **h** hoot **i** one **j** hen **k** rough **l** aid **m** tick

Unit 55

1 trip, present, throw, aid, piece, edge, choose, dark, loud, contain

2 undo, unclear, unpack, unlock, unfold, unfair, untidy, unlucky, unafraid, uncover, unsure, unblocked

Unit 56

1 bikes, animals, paths, princesses, teachers, children, hobbies, bananas, octopuses, eyelashes, waltzes, monkeys, teeth, boxes, shelves

2 **a** been **b** hair **c** hear **d** stopped **e** hurried **f** arrived **g** helpful

3 centre/edge, outside/inside, odd/even, weak/ strong, small/large, hurry/rush, amaze/ surprise, loud/noisy, answer/reply, glitter/sparkle

> **Synonyms** are words with the same or similar meanings.

> **Small** and **little** are synonyms. They have the same meaning.
> **Frighten** and **scare** are synonyms too.

1   Match the words from the box with their synonyms.

hit   allow   tear   centre   stone   scare
blend   sparkle   twist   odd

frighten ....scare............

glitter ....

curl ....

strange ....

rock ....

strike ....

middle ....

permit ....

rip ....

mix ....

> **Antonyms** are words with opposite meanings.

> **Tiny** and **huge** are antonyms. They have opposite meanings.
> **Go to sleep** and **wake up** are antonyms too.

2   Match the words from the box with their antonyms.

enter   dry   strong   near   top   over
never   short   outside   friend

under ....over............

weak ....

leave ....

wet ....

bottom ....

long ....

inside ....

enemy ....

far ....

always ....

Past tense verbs	
Drop the "e" and add "ed" to regular verbs.	
smile	**smiled**
tape	**taped**

1 Add "ed" to the following verbs.

chase .... _chased_ ....   live ....

wave ....   arrive ....

amaze ....   snore ....

like ....   invite ....

hate ....   share ....

decide ....   rescue ....

prepare ....   agree ....

2 Add "ed" to the following verbs.

a (score) I ...... _scored_ .... the winning goal yesterday.

b (close) The entries .... last Friday.

c (smile) Todd .... when he was announced the winner.

d (paste) We .... the pictures in our books.

e (use) Kelly .... a nail to hang her picture.

Unit 30

Look out for common letter patterns. The letter pattern "br" is found in many words.

1 Circle all the words in the snake which start with the letter pattern "br". Write them below.

breadbitbridgebreakbakerbrushranchbranchbrothertherebrownbroomsentbravetrapbrickbowbrunchmegnunchbride

(bread)

.... bread ....

....

....

....

2 Choose the correct "br" word from the box to complete the sentences.

bring   breakfast   bread   ~~broccoli~~

a My favorite vegetable is ...._broccoli_......

b I usually have cereal for ....

c Be sure to .... your swimsuit when you come to my house tomorrow.

d My mother bakes fresh .... every Saturday.

Unit 31

Adding "ing" to verbs ending in "y"	
For actions happening now, keep the "y" and add "ing".	
fry	I'm **frying** an egg now.
pay	She's **paying** for the new hat now.

1 Add "ing" to the following verbs.

try ....*trying*...........   fly ....

spray ....   say ....

lay ....   tidy ....

bury ....   copy ....

obey ....   pray ....

enjoy ....   stay ....

worry ....   hurry ....

carry ....   spy ....

2 Add "ing" to the following verbs.

a (fry) Mom is .....*frying*..... eggs for breakfast.

b (empty) Be careful when you are .... the pan of hot water.

c (dry) The paintings are .... in the sun.

d (terrify) This story is .... me!

e (annoy) You are .... the cat! Stop it!

Unit 32

> **Homophones** are words that sound the same, but have different spellings and different meanings.
>
> | sea/see | The **sea** was calm. |
> |---|---|
> | | I can't **see** anything because it's dark. |

1   Choose the correct word to complete the sentences.

a (rode/road) The ....*road*........ was very bumpy.

b (rode/road) Isabelle .... the black pony.

c (tale/tail) Dad read us the .... of the green monster last night.

d (tale/tail) The cat's .... was long with black and white stripes.

e (ate/eight) We .... all the ripe strawberries we could find.

f (ate/eight) There will be .... candles on Carla's cake.

g (blue/blew) Cameron won the .... ribbon in the running race.

h (blue/blew) The wind .... strongly all night.

i (read/red) I .... that book last week.

j (read/red) The .... car belongs to Mr Lee.

k (hair / hare) My .... is full of knots.

l (hair / hare) The .... was eating the lettuce leaves.

Writing

2   Rewrite the sentence with all words spelled correctly.

My dog has a lot of trubble with flees.

....

For verbs ending with a vowel followed by "y", add "s" for he/she and "ed" for past tense.

Spray	He/She **sprays**	I **sprayed** it yesterday.
Stay	He/She **stays**	She **stayed** here last night.

1   Add "s" and "ed" to the following verbs.

verb	"s"	"ed"
stay	stays	stayed
enjoy		
obey		
play		
bray		
display		

For verbs ending with a consonant followed by "y", change the "y" to "i" and add "es" or "ed".

Dry	He/She **dries**	She **dried** her hair.
Cry	He/She **cries**	They **cried** during the movie.

2   Add "es" and "ed" to the following verbs.

verb	"es"	"ed"
cry	cries	cried
try		
bury		
carry		
hurry		
worry		
copy		

Measurement word search

Find the measurements words listed in the box. Write each word on the lines.

length	area	volume	~~mass~~	temperature	time	centimeter
capacity	liter	kilogram	lighter	heavier	warmer	cooler

t	h	c	a	p	a	c	i	t	y
e	e	v	h	w	a	r	m	e	r
m	a	r	g	o	l	l	k	a	r
p	v	n	r	e	l	o	o	c	j
e	i	o	j	f	r	e	t	i	l
r	e	t	e	m	i	t	n	e	c
a	r	e	m	a	s	s	n	s	w
t	o	r	e	t	h	g	i	l	t
u	a	r	e	a	t	n	s	i	s
r	r	t	g	h	t	a	m	h	t
e	m	u	l	o	v	e	n	a	s

mass

....

....

....

....

....

....

....

....

....

....

....

"ed" and "ing"		
For words ending with a vowel followed by a consonant, double the consonant. Then add "ed" or "ing".		
mop	mopped	mopping
knit	knitted	knitting
skip	skipped	skipping

I shouldn't have mentioned the captain's bad breath!

1 **Add "ed" and "ing" to the following verbs.**

verb	"ed"	"ing"
skip	skipped	skipping
flip	....	....
trip	....	....
shop	....	....
step	....	....
chip	....	....
spot	....	....
drum	....	....
snap	....	....
hug	....	....
rip	....	....
stop	....	....

English has many common letter patterns. The letter pattern "ee" is found in many words.

1 Circle all the words in the snake which contain the letter pattern "ee". Write them below.

sleepcuddleebetweeninecheesethesemeetkeepbyqueenvesecanteennonameeagreeeagereastdeepwarmweedkitiekeen

.............snake............. ....

....

....

....

2 Choose the correct "ee" word from the box to complete the sentences.

need ~~feed~~ reef free cheetah

a We were in time to see the attendant ....feed........

the ....

b You will .... a ticket to enter.

c I saw a coral .... from the boat.

d I didn't have to pay for the pen. It was ....

Add the endings shown to the verbs.

verb	"ed"	"s" or "es"	"ing"
crash	crashed	crashes	crashing
wrap			
fry			
bake			
smile			
hurry			
drag			
enjoy			
share			
fly			
carry			
pass			
trip			
plan			
expect			
jump			

Community word search

Find the community words listed in the box. Write each word on the lines.

council	town	church	city	library	hall	school
shop	park	~~gardens~~	hospital	cinema	pool	

p	m	g	a	r	d	e	n	s	m
v	o	l	i	b	r	a	r	y	t
a	r	o	b	a	l	m	w	m	e
c	h	a	l	l	m	a	d	r	p
h	c	h	c	i	t	y	v	l	a
u	u	r	s	m	c	z	m	q	r
r	t	m	w	h	t	n	g	n	k
c	s	c	h	o	o	l	u	w	g
h	k	l	a	t	i	p	s	o	h
m	s	c	i	n	e	m	a	t	c

gardens

....

....

....

....

....

....

....

....

....

....

....

Unit 39

Adjectives
For nouns ending with two consonants, add "y" to form adjectives.

luck – **lucky**   box – **boxy**
rock – **rocky**   wind – **windy**

1   Add "y" to the following words.

wind .... *windy* ....   sand ....

trick ....   dust ....

hair ....   soap ....

sugar ....   salt ....

sleep ....   pluck ....

frost ....   rust ....

thirst ....   lump ....

wood ....   cheer ....

2   Add "y" to the following verbs.

a   (cloud) It was a very ...... *cloudy* .... day.

b   (blood) Gemma's knees were .... after she fell off her bike.

c   (itch) My skin is very .... under the cast.

d   (dirt) After the soccer game, Jim's uniform was ....

e   (fish) There was a .... smell coming from the fridge.

Find the jobs listed in the box. Write each word on the lines.

~~mayor~~	dentist	teacher	farmer	nurse	driver
police	doctor	builder	mechanic	chef	plumber	miner

c	h	c	h	a	m	o	s	t	m
m	r	e	n	i	m	a	y	o	f
t	e	a	c	h	e	r	y	p	f
s	d	m	p	g	c	m	d	o	a
i	l	r	l	e	h	t	s	l	r
t	i	o	u	s	a	c	i	i	m
n	u	t	m	r	n	b	h	c	e
e	b	c	b	u	i	l	d	e	r
d	m	o	e	n	c	d	m	o	f
h	b	d	r	i	v	e	r	m	y

.... *mayor* ....

....

....

....

....

....

....

....

....

....

....

Adjectives
For many nouns ending with a vowel followed by a consonant, double the consonant. Then add "y" to form an adjective.
fun – **funny**   fog – **foggy**

1   **Double the final consonant before adding "y" to the following words.**

spot   ....*spotty*..........   bag   ....

star   ....   mud   ....

grub   ....   smog   ....

run   ....   zip   ....

knot   ....   nip   ....

slop   ....   star   ....

2   **Add "y" to the following words.**

a   (snap) Mrs. Gibbon's dog is very ....*snappy*......

b   (bog) The ground here is very ....

c   (fun) The .... movie had everyone laughing.

d   (blur) I can't see the boy in the photo beacuse it

....

Synonyms are words with the same or similar meanings.

Strong and powerful are synonyms. They have the same meaning.
Delicious and tasty are synonyms too.

1 Match the words from the box with their synonyms.

amaze	collect	lock	weep
least	~~powerful~~	tired	raise

strong ....powerful.......

bolt ....

sleepy ....

lift ....

surprise ....

gather ....

smallest ....

cry ....

Antonyms are words with opposite meanings.

Strong and weak are antonyms. They have opposite meanings.
Drop and catch are antonyms too.

2 Match the words from the box with their antonyms.

happy	present	wrong	~~catch~~	on
sunset	shallow	shout	laugh	mend

drop ....catch.........

cry ....

sad ....

right ....

sunrise ....

deep ....

whisper ....

break ....

off ....

absent ....

Adjectives with "ful"
When adding "full" to change a noun to an adjective, drop the last "l".
care – **careful**   harm – **harmful**
fear – **fearful**   cheer – **cheerful**

1   Add "full" to the following words.

cheer   + full   = ...*cheerful*....   boast   + full   = ...

use   + full   = ...   thought + full   = ...

hope   + full   = ...   joy   + full   = ...

power   + full   = ...   pain   + full   = ...

respect + full   = ...   truth   + full   = ...

watch   + full   = ...   peace   + full   = ...

play   + full   = ...   grace   + full   = ...

forget   + full   = ...   thank   + full   = ...

2   Add "full" to the following words or parts of words.

a   (help) "It would be ....*helpful*....... if you could collect the book," said Mrs. Hagen.

b   (harm) The sun can be .... to your skin.

c   (faith) My dog is very ....

d   (fork) Jason picked up a big .... of peas.

e   (wonder) My friend gave me a .... birthday present.

Look out for common letter patterns. The letter pattern "oa" is found in many words.

1 Circle all the words in the snake which contain the letter pattern "oa". Write them below.

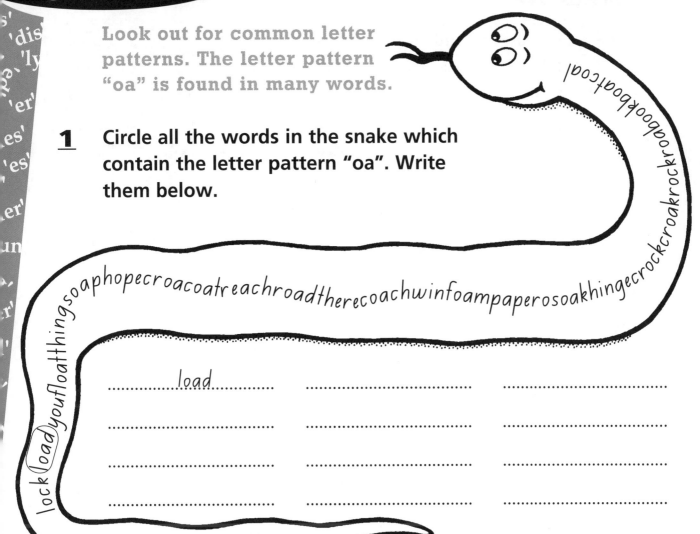

................load................ ....

....

....

....

2 Choose the correct "oa" word from the box to complete the sentences.

| goal ~~loaf~~ goat roast moan |

a My grandfather once ate a ....loaf.......... of bread in less than an hour.

b Jessie got one .... in her soccer game yesterday.

c Tim let out a .... as the .... kicked him in the stomach.

d We had .... beef for dinner for Dad's birthday.

Adding "er" and "est"

Comparative and superlative adjectives		
For adjectives ending in "y", change the "y" to "i", then add "er" or "est".		
happy	**happier**	**happiest**
dry	**drier**	**driest**

The sun has made my skin like leather!

Add "er" and "est" to the following words.

word	"er"	"est"
happy	*happier*	*happiest*
dirty	....	....
funny	....	....
soapy	....	....
muddy	....	....
sticky	....	....
baggy	....	....
thirsty	....	....
silly	....	....
sleepy	....	....
lucky	....	....
tricky	....	....

Homophones are words that sound the same, but have different spellings and different meanings.	
ate/eight	We **ate** fish for lunch. The show begins at **eight** o'clock.
flower/flour	My sister works at a **flower** shop. I have to buy **flour** at the supermarket.

1 Choose the correct word to complete the sentences.

a (flower/flour) This ....*flower*........ is a rose.

b (flower/flour) The .... is in the cupboard.

c (wear/where) I think I will .... my red jumper today.

d (wear/where) Can you tell me .... the library is?

e (write/right) The bus turned .... at the traffic lights.

f (write/right) "........................... your name at the top of the page," said Mrs. Evans.

g (cheep/cheap) We could hear the .... of the baby bird.

h (cheep/cheap) At the one-dollar shop, everything is ....

i (main/mane) The supermarket is on the .... street.

j (main/mane) The horse's .... flew out behind as it ran across the field.

Writing

2 Rewrite the sentence with all words spelled correctly.

I'm not aloud to come to the party on Tuseday.

....

Adding "ly"

Adverbs
Adverbs describe verbs. Add "ly" to many adjectives to form adverbs.
bad – **badly**   clear – **clearly**
slow – **slowly**   wild – **wildly**

I badly need some chocolate!

1   Add "ly" to the following words.

slow ....*slowly*.......... quick ....

soft .... neat ....

bright .... thin ....

weak .... loose ....

bold .... brave ....

correct .... clever ....

careful .... sudden ....

strong .... clear ....

2   Add "ly" to the following verbs.

a   (wild) The boat was tossed ....*wildly*....... on the rough sea.

b   (glum) Nadia stared .... at the broken jar.

c   (gruff) The monster spoke .... His voice didn't sound friendly.

d   (hopeful) Timothy looked .... in the freezer for some more ice cream.

e   (proud) Her parents watched .... as Claire played the piano.

Time word search

Find the time words listed in the box. Write each word on the lines.

minute	hour	clock	half	digital	start	finish	week
month	year	midnight	midday	~~calendar~~			

c	a	l	e	n	d	a	r	w	m
l	l	f	h	e	i	e	e	e	o
o	c	o	l	w	g	r	e	a	t
c	u	r	c	m	i	n	u	t	e
r	e	r	m	k	t	i	e	w	y
c	t	t	o	h	a	l	f	e	a
l	r	b	n	a	l	t	a	e	d
o	a	v	t	d	i	r	g	k	d
c	t	h	h	s	i	n	i	f	i
h	s	t	h	g	i	n	d	i	m

.... *calendar* ....

....

....

....

....

....

....

....

....

....

....

....

We will never make it in time!

49

Unit 49

Contractions	
have + not = **haven't**	did + not = **didn't**
is + not = **isn't**	he + is = **he's**

1 Join the words to form contractions.

is   + not = ...*isn't*........   was   + not   = ...

did   + not = ...   have + not   = ...

must + not = ...   were + not   = ...

I   + am = ...   I   + have = ...

here + is   = ...   there + is   = ...

2 Circle the correct contraction.

a	<u>She is</u> going on holidays today.	She'is	(She's)	Shes'
b	<u>I have</u> left my lunch at home?	Iha've	I'ave	I've
c	<u>There is</u> our bus.	There's	Ther's	The'res
d	Rachael <u>has not</u> arrived yet.	has'nt	hasn't	has'not
e	<u>He will</u> be here soon.	He'll	He'ill	Hew'ill
f	<u>That is</u> the end of the story.	Tha's	That's'	That's

Find the food words listed in the box. Write the words on the lines.

pear	banana	corn	bread	peanut	tomato	lemon
~~bean~~	meat	milk	cheese	jelly	juice	carrot

t	o	m	y	t	o	t	a	e	m
o	b	e	a	n	i	u	e	m	i
c	a	r	r	o	t	c	m	y	l
a	o	t	a	m	o	t	t	o	k
r	c	r	m	e	y	r	i	d	a
p	h	w	n	l	f	m	t	a	r
e	e	h	c	r	y	l	l	e	j
a	e	j	u	i	c	e	j	r	e
r	s	m	a	n	a	n	a	b	l
m	e	p	e	a	n	u	t	l	y

.... *bean* ....

....

....

....

....

....

....

....

....

....

....

I don't like tomato.

Silent letters
Many English words contain silent letters.
crumb (silent **b**)   **knife** (silent **k**)
calf (silent **l**)   **sign** (silent **g**)

1   **Circle the silent letter in each of the words in the box.**

lam**b**   write   ghost   climb   knee   comb   half   wreck
hour   thumb   knock   numb   guess   bomb   gnaw   limb

2   **Write the words that contain a silent "b" on the line below.**

lamb ....

....

3   **Match the words from Exercise 1 to the meanings below.**

50% of something
half ....

to destroy ....

a joint in your leg..........................

to estimate ....

from one o'clock to two o'clock

is an ....

a baby sheep ....

to rap on a door............................

to chew ....

to put letters on paper with a
pencil or pen

....

an explosive ....

a tree branch ....

without feeling ....

something used to make your hair

look nice ....

a short inner finger ....

to go up a ladder, stairs, or mountain

....

a spirit ....

Look out for common letter
patterns. The letter pattern
"ai" is found in many words.

1 Circle all the words in the snake which contain
the letter pattern "ai". Write them below.

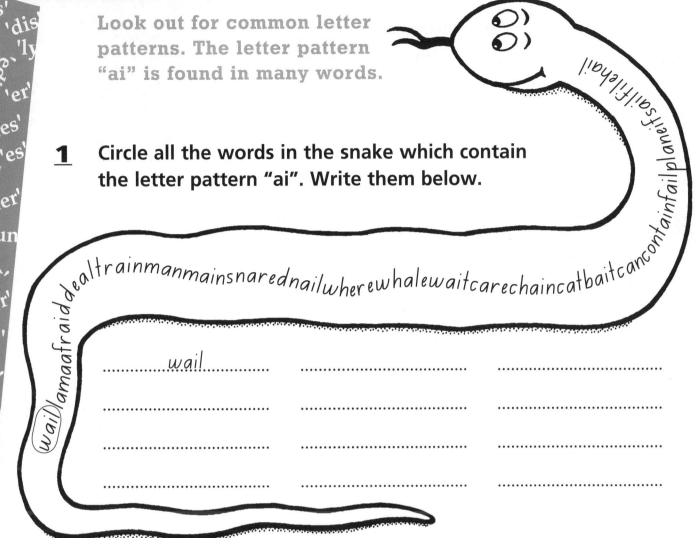

..........*wail*.......... ....

....

....

....

2 Choose the correct "ai" word from the box to complete the
sentences.

mail sailed stain ~~rain~~ train remained trail

a The ....*rain*.......... washed away the .... of footprints.

b .... comes to my town by ....

c The ketchup .... on Jim's shirt .... there even
after he washed it three times.

d The yacht .... into the harbor.

Compound words

Compound words
Two small words can sometimes form one bigger word.
bath + room = **bathroom**
bed + room = **bedroom**
life + time = **lifetime**

I love my bedroom!

1 **Join the smaller words to form compound words.**

bath   + room   = ...*bathroom*.........

flash   + light   = ...

work   + book   = ...

finger   + nail   = ...

over   + coat   = ...

life   + boat   = ...

sun   + glasses = ...

button + hole   = ...

sun   + burn   = ...

home + work   = ...

tooth + brush = ...

foot   + print   = ...

flag   + pole   = ...

rain   + coat   = ...

life   + saver   = ...

sand   + paper   = ...

2 **Use the compound words in Exercise 1 to answer the questions.**

a Which two compound words contain the word "life"?
.................*lifeboat*................. ....

b Which two compound words contain the word "work"?
....

c Which two compound words contain the word "coat"?
....

3 **Unjumble the letters and solve the compound word sum.**

(ote) .... + nail = ...

Finding small words inside bigger words	
age in **stage**	**mat** in **tomato**
car and **go** in **cargo**	**me** in **America**

Find the smaller words in the words in bold.

a   Find a number in **often**.   *ten*

b   Find part of a shark in **finish**.

c   Find a word for "boy" in **ladder**.

d   Find a word for battle in **warn**.

e   Find an animal in **shape**.

f   Find a word for "friend" in **pale**.

g   Find part of a bird in **swing**.

h   Find the sound an owl makes in **shoot**.

i   Find a number in **shone**.

j   Find a bird in **kitchen**.

k   Find the opposite of "smooth" in **through**.

l   Find help in **laid**.

m   Find the sound a clock makes in **stick**.

> **Synonyms** are words with the same or similar meanings.
>
> **Amaze** and **surprise** are synonyms. They have the same meaning.
> **Toss** and **throw** are synonyms too.

1 **Match the words from the box with their synonyms.**

dark	contain	aid	loud	edge	throw
	~~trip~~	piece	present	choose	

outing ....*trip*.........   gift ....

toss ....   help ....

bit ....   border ....

pick ....   gloomy ....

noisy ....   hold ....

> **Antonyms** are words with different meanings. Some antonyms are formed by adding "un" to the beginning of a word.
>
> **Unhappy** is an antonym for **happy**
> **Unlock** is a synonym for **lock**

2 **Write the antonyms formed by adding "un" to the beginning of the following words.**

do ....*undo*........   clear ....

pack ....   lock ....

fold ....   fair ....

tidy ....   lucky ....

afraid ....   cover ....

sure ....   blocked ....

1   **Write the plurals of each of these words.**

bike .... *bikes* ....   animal ....   path ....

princess ....   teacher ....   child ....

hobby ....   banana ....   octopus ....

eyelash ....   waltz ....   monkey ....

tooth ....   box ....   shelf ....

2   **Circle the correct word.**

a   I have never (bean / (been)) to Alice Springs.

b   You should comb your (hair / hare).

c   Did you (hear / here) the bell?

d   Ben (stoped / stopped) the ball with his foot.

e   Everyone (hurried / hurryed) inside when it began to rain.

f   My cousins (arriveed / arrivd / arrived) last night.

g   That's not very (helpfull / helpful).

3   **Draw lines to join the pairs of words.**

Antonyms		Synomyms	
center	even	hurry	reply
outside	edge	amaze	sparkle
odd	inside	loud	rush
weak	large	answer	noisy
small	strong	glitter	surprise

OXFORD
UNIVERSITY PRESS

198 Madison Avenue
New York, NY 10016 USA

Great Clarendon Street, Oxford OX2 6DP UK

Oxford University Press is a department of the University of Oxford.
It furthers the University's objective of excellence in research,
scholarship, and education by publishing worldwide in

Oxford   New York

Auckland   Cape Town   Dar es Salaam   Hong Kong   Karachi
Kuala Lumpur   Madrid   Melbourne   Mexico City   Nairobi
New Delhi   Shanghai   Taipei   Toronto

With offices in

Argentina   Austria   Brazil   Chile   Czech Republic   France   Greece
Guatemala   Hungary   Italy   Japan   Poland   Portugal   Singapore
South Korea   Switzerland   Thailand   Turkey   Ukraine   Vietnam

OXFORD and OXFORD ENGLISH are registered trademarks of
Oxford University Press.

© Oxford University Press 2008

Originally published by Oxford University Press Australia in 2005

This edition is adapted by arrangement with Oxford University Press
Australia and licensed for sale in Korea and the rest of the world,
but excluding the US, UK, Australia and New Zealand, and for
export therefrom.

Database right Oxford University Press (maker)

Market Development Director, Asia: Chris Balderston
Managing Editor, Asia: Barnaby Pelter
Project Manager, Editorial, Production, Design: Allison Harm
Manufacturing Manager: Shanta Persaud
Manufacturing Controller: Eve Wong

ISBN: 978 0 19 478300 2

Printed in China

Printing (last digit) 10   9   8   7   6   5   4   3   2   1

We would like to thank the following for permission to reproduce the cover
photograph: Tourism Queensland, Australia: Mark Nissen, Fish And
Coral in the Great Barrier Reef.